PREFACE

I have always been a morning person, but there was something different about this day. It was the spring of 2004. I was 30 years old, with a wife and a young son. Somehow along the way, I had learned a valuable lesson about the importance of time. As I once told a co-worker, "It's never about money and always about time." This had become my new mantra as I gazed out of my apartment complex window at four in the morning with blurred vision and cloudy thoughts, looking at the empty interstate leading into Washington, D.C. For two months, I had been attempting to capitalize on my limited amount of time and do what I had seen few do—follow one's dreams.

The small business environment has always felt second nature to me, from my earlier fascination of tales of small business success to my enterprising efforts I pursued as a kid. In high school, I was always following the next big idea and in college had a breakthrough with my own nonprofit organization, the Young Entrepreneurs Program (YEP) (www.yep4youth.org). Yet somehow *The Entrepreneurial Spirit*, which had lived deep within me from early on, had taken a backseat to working for advertising agencies, media companies, and dot-coms. So there I stood in the wee hours of the morning, looking out of the window with this burning desire to create something new. In those days, the idea was in its infancy, but maybe this new company would be one created for entrepreneurs by someone that knew the environment well. Somehow I knew that what I was working toward had nothing to do with climbing the corporate ladder or becoming ridiculously wealthy or even famous. Instead, I was pursuing a life that would provide me with more time, more control, and more happiness. Sure, more money would be nice. In pursuing my own dream then, maybe, I could show others how to do the same as well.

In my effort to create this new company, I would wake up at roughly five (or earlier) each morning, fire up the coffee pot, and make my way to my desk. It was there in those quiet hours that I would begin grinding out my business ideas and dreams over a homemade cup o' Joe. This daily, sleep-deprived ritual of coffee and business became my comfort zone of sorts, a place of peace and quiet in what was sure to be a hectic day. For me, it was usually the only time during the day that I could get some constructive work done toward achieving my goals. So it was only natural that when I decided to name my company that I named it after the moment and place in time where business and coffee converged. Thus The Entrepreneur Café, LLC, was born.

> *The Entrepreneurial Spirit, which had always lived within me had somehow taken a back seat.*

One thing stands out about that particular morning as I gazed out of the large windows overlooking the nation's capital—the image of the person looking back at me! Instead of seeing the groggy mirror-image reflection of myself, I saw an older, wiser, and future successful version of myself. Somehow the guy that I was looking at had found a way to not bail but to stick with his dreams, even during the hard times. This future version of me had taken on the critics, pushing past nonbelievers and naysayers, to build a company that would change the lives of countless individuals both inside and outside of the small business world.

As I reflect on my own experiences, I can honestly say that *The Entrepreneurial Spirit Lives*. It exists in all of us as that voice heard ever so subtly or deeply that won't seem to let your dreams die. And so it is with small business dreams in mind that the book *The Entrepreneurial Spirit . . . Lives*. It is with great pleasure that I welcome you to The Entrepreneur Café, LLC. As you read through this book, I invite you to fire up your own coffee pot, pull up a proverbial chair, get comfortable, and explore how The Entrepreneur Café, LLC, can be of service to you. May this book be the start of all of your small business dreams coming true.

Sincerely,

Cavanaugh L. Gray
Founder and Director of Business Development
The Entrepreneur Café, LLC

INTRODUCTION

For as long as I can remember, I have been fascinated by entrepreneurship. Before the word *entrepreneur* was trendy or mainstream, it was the occupation that only crazy folks were willing to pursue. Only a person who wasn't sane would forego a possible lifetime of job security and a steady paycheck for the very distant mirage of small business success. Some 30 years ago, entrepreneurial glory was reserved for those with last names like Gates, Jobs, or Dell. However, today is a new day and no longer is the term *entrepreneur* misunderstood. For many of us, small business ownership has become a goal that we aspire to—the new American Dream.

What I remember most about my own love affair with small business are the tales of courageous men and women willing to risk it all on a chance to see their small business dreams come true. Something about those stories struck a chord with me early on, and, looking back now, it's clear to see that I was destined to be an entrepreneur. From my days of running small enterprises as a kid, to my first real successful venture as a collegian with the nonprofit organization the Young Entrepreneurs Program, and now as the Founder and Director of Business Development for The Entrepreneur Café, LLC, I have always known that this is what I was meant to do. I am proud of the role that I have been able to play in the lives of countless individuals as they have looked to pursue their own dreams. It's a job that I don't take lightly at The Entrepreneur Café, LLC.

According to the U.S. Census Bureau, there are an estimated 27.9 million small firms operating in the United States. Of that number, an estimated 21.7 million are one-person shops with no employees where the owner often wears every hat in the building. At some point along the way, this army of small business owners had to look in the mirror and ask themselves the million-dollar question, "Why do I want to go into business for myself?" This question is critical to the success of any enterprise, and so I pose it to you: **Why do you want to go into business for yourself?** Do you desire to make more money? Have you longed for more time over

Small business ownership has become the new American Dream.

your present schedule? Do you wish that you could take more control over your career and your future? Or do you see small business ownership as your own yellow brick road to happiness? All are excellent reasons, but it could very well be none of these choices. Maybe it's that nagging feeling that hasn't gone away or that voice that seems to scream out that you were put here to do something greater. It could be the feeling that you should be completing a task started a long time ago that if it goes undone by you, it will never get done! If this is where you find yourself, then this book is definitely for you.

Small businesses usually fall into one of three categories; I will start with the latter two.

In the middle of this spectrum are those companies that fall into the *expansion category*. These companies were founded on the grit and determination of the owners and have survived off of pure momentum for several years only to find themselves in a place of stagnation with company operations having plateaued.

To the far right of this spectrum are the *growth companies* that have managed to move past the expansion phase and now have visions of being mentioned in the same category as Facebook, Amazon, and Google. Their goals center on scaling up their staff, opening multiple locations, or pursuing the elusive initial public offering.

To the left of this spectrum are the *start-ups.* These are usually individuals and small companies in the preliminary stages of their small business efforts. At this stage, they are usually trying to get a better handle on their own ideas and looking to navigate company formation and just gain basic insight as to what their enterprise will look like going forward. Also at this stage, many owners find themselves wrestling with similar business issues, including a lack of managerial experience, ineffective marketing, a lack of financing options, and an inability to locate resources that will help them start, grow, and succeed.

I wrote *The Entrepreneurial Spirit Lives* with the start-up in mind. Each topic in the book is taken either from a question posed by an early-stage business owner or from a real-life business case that The Entrepreneur Café, LLC, has worked on over the years. In short, this book is a resource for practical issues related to small business management, marketing, and finances—all in laymen's terms. I also wrote this book with your life in mind and an understanding that with professional, family, and personal obligations, none of us has unlimited time. Many of us suffer from information overload, so I don't expect you to have to read through an encyclopedia before you can get to the heart of the business issues most pressing to you.

Lastly, I wrote this book with the intent of helping entrepreneurs theoretically grasp the subject matter and then practically apply it to their own businesses all in a matter of three to five easy steps.

Thank you for your support of The Entrepreneur Café, LLC, and be sure to let us know how *The Entrepreneurial Spirit Lives* has helped your business efforts. Email me at cgray@ecafellc.com.

ACKNOWLEDGEMENTS

To a God who makes this and all things possible.

To my amazing family ...

To my beautiful wife, Akua, thank you for walking with me on this journey.

To my two copilots, Gabriel and William, all that I do is so that you will know a different future!

To my great-grandmother, Mary L. Joyce; my grandfather, Mitchell Gaddis; my dad, Wilbert J. Gray; my mother, Linda D. Gaddis; my brother, Mitchell L. Gaddis; and to the rest of my family ... thank you for your love and support over the years.

To entrepreneurs everywhere, nurturing a dream!

COPYRIGHT

THE ENTREPRENEURIAL SPIRIT LIVES
Published by The Entrepreneur Café, LLC
715 W. 15th Street
Chicago, IL 60607
phone/fax 877-511-4820
cgray@ecafellc.com
www.ecafellc.com

Library of Congress Cataloging-in-Publication Data
Gray, Cavanaugh L.-1st ed.
ISBN: 978-0-9855668-0-7

Front cover Illustration by Darryl Jones of Splattered Ink.
Copies of The Entrepreneurial Spirit Lives are available at special quantity discounts for use as gifts, promotions, book clubs, and business trainings. For more information contact The Entrepreneur Café, LLC, at 877-511-4820 or visit our website at www.ecafellc.com.

END OF CHAPTER EXERCISES

UNDERSTANDING THE ICONS

WHAT IS MANAGEMENT?

Management is the alignment and coordination of multiple activities associated with running a company for the purpose of accomplishing a desired goal and objective. Many small businesses struggle due to an inexperienced management team. When you see this icon, it indicates that you are working on an exercise that will help you to make more productive managerial decisions.

WHAT IS MARKETING?

Marketing is the process of creating and delivering goods and services to customers and all of the activities associated with gaining new customers and retaining loyal customers. The marketing discipline cuts across multiple areas of a company's business and is integral to the organization's overall success. When you see this icon, it indicates that you will be working on an exercise that will help you to create more low-to-no-cost marketing that will lead to greater returns for your organization.

WHAT IS FINANCE?

Financial management for a small business involves managing resources for the purpose of achieving a desired financial objective. Some key financial objectives include wealth creation for the business, generating cash flows, financing options, financial reporting, and budgeting. When you see this icon, it indicates that you will be working on an exercise that will assist you in making the best possible financial decisions for your organization.

WHAT ARE RESOURCES?

Business resources are anything that helps a company operate and conduct business for a profit. The effective management of business resources could be a strong indicator of companies operating at a higher level versus those that are not. When you see this icon, it indicates that you are working with informational resources that will help you develop new business ideas, network and share resources with other entrepreneurs. These resources are geared at addressing specific management, marketing, and financial obstacles that could be slowing your business down.

CONTENTS

1. Life Planning Helps You Start Your Business Off Right

2. Secrets of Small Business Success

3. A Closer Look at Business Plans

4. Which Incorporation Is Right for You?

5. Owners Should Exercise Caution When Partnering

6. Mission Statements Keep Your Business on Course

7. Give Me an Hour and Some Crayons, and I'll Give You a Business

8. Resolutions for Small Business Success

9. For Quality Advice, Advisory Boards Can't Be Overlooked

10. Analysis Is Key to Outwitting the Competition

11. Operating a Business on the Cheap

12. Sparking Small Business Creativity

13. Crafting a Confidentiality Agreement

14. Making Policy Manuals Work for Your Small Business

15. Maneuvering Small Business Manufacturing

16. Business Owners Should Be Prepared to Defend Themselves

17. Can Southern Illinois Become the Napa Valley of the Midwest?

18. The Art of Business Networking

19. Public Relations Done Right

20. To Get Good at Advertising, Know the Formula

21. Setting Prices

22. Emerging Markets Provide Answers for Entrepreneurs

23. For Today's Entrepreneurs, It's Hip to Be Square

24. Taking a Step Back from Business Planning

25. Social Entrepreneurs Look to Fundraising to Grow

"Many men fail because they quit too soon. They lose faith when the signs are against them. They do not have the courage to hold on, to keep fighting in spite of that which seems insurmountable. If more of us would strike out and attempt the impossible, we very soon would find the truth of that old saying that nothing is impossible . . . Abolish fear and you can accomplish anything you wish."

—Dr. C.E. Welch (1922)

THE
ENTREPRENEURIAL
SPIRIT LIVES

1

Life Planning Helps You Start Your Business Off Right

Going into 2003, I was expecting my first son. As the New Year approached, I found myself thinking about life in a whole new way. Before this, my thoughts were of my corporate life and of leisure activities. What I thought were resolutions at the time were much bigger and more life changing than I had realized and the primary reasons that The Entrepreneur Café, LLC, exists today. Back then, I was working a corporate job but found no joy in it. I was spending more hours at my desk than I cared to and wishing all the while that I could be at home hanging out with my son. Looking back, what I truly desired was more time to spend with those I loved most, greater control over my schedule, more joy and fulfillment in my days, and the opportunity to impact the world. I knew that I wouldn't get to where I wanted to be without facing some tough questions. In doing so, I would uncover answers that would alter the rest of my life.

Developing a life plan is a process to help you better identify your personal and professional priorities. A decade ago owners started businesses with a success-at-all-cost approach, which leaves little time for much else. Today many entrepreneurs are starting businesses and running them in a manner that fits their lifestyle and provides them with an improved quality of life. If you are just starting out in business, a life plan can help guide you through the developmental stages so that you build a company that makes you happy and is in step with how you live. If you happen to be well established, then a life plan could be your reality check.

When I sat down to do my life plan, I was looking to better define myself as an entrepreneur and build a structure for how I would run The Entrepreneur Café, LLC. One of the first things that came to mind centered on my core values. My core values included hard work, valuing people, and having an impact on my community. My great-grandmother raised me and taught me many of the great lessons that I was able to lean on later in life when building a foundation for my business.

Today entrepreneurs are running businesses in a manner that fits their lifestyle.

I'm also a firm believer that a dream and determination can take you a long way. At this stage in life, what is it that you *dream* about? Has your day-to-day become mundane or routine? Thankfully, I still dream with the same anything-is-possible attitude that I had when I was a kid. One of the toughest things I face in business these days is when I encounter someone who, because of life's circumstances, has stopped dreaming or simply forgotten how.

The next question is an important litmus test of where you might be in life right now. Are you currently having *fun*? Or put another way … are you *happy*? If you are a business proprietor, the answer to this question might change by the second according to the way the economy goes. But I urge you to ask the question and then be patient enough to wait for an honest answer.

When I started working on my life plan, my list of personal questions was pretty exhaustive as I pondered the type of employees and work environment I wanted to have, what my financial goals were, and how my small efforts would impact the world around me. As a result of this process, I now live a life centered around my faith, my family, and my impact on other people's lives. And, oh yeah, I happen to run a company that gives me the freedom to be actively involved in all of those things.

Whether you are already in business and planning your company's next steps or just setting out, I encourage you to set the resolutions aside and try developing a life plan. Earlier I asked if you were happy in your current occupation, business, or the manner in which you run your business. If not, what questions do you need to ask and what changes do you need to make so that things turn out amazingly different in the upcoming year?

Developing Your Life Plan

Not sure where to begin in building your business? Start by developing a life plan. Download the complete Life Planning Questionnaire from The Entrepreneur Café, LLC, website at www.ecafellc.com/resources.

Take some time to thoroughly go through and give some honest thought to these questions. My hope is that it will provide you with the insight you need to move your business dreams forward.

2

Secrets of Small Business Success

Why is it so hard to decide what type of business to start up? I've always heard you must start a business that you love doing and are good at. I understand this concept and agree with it, but I don't feel like I'm great at anything but rather a "jack-of-all-trades." Do you have any suggestions that might keep me on the right track?

Your question strikes at the heart of what every entrepreneur wants to know and that is, *What is the winning formula for developing a successful small business?* Although there is no magic formula for getting it right, successful individuals seem to have traveled similar paths and have had similar experiences. A closer look at the following points should help bring a little more clarity to what it is that you are looking to do.

Do What You Love

The old saying is, "Do what you love and you will never work a day in your life." Something to keep in mind is that a large number of businesses start off as hobbies. Recently, my sister-in-law, who has a knack for arts and crafts and the creative, mentioned that she had begun making custom T-shirts for herself and wearing them to work.

It wasn't long before her creative designs caught the attention of her coworkers, and she started taking orders. Just that quickly her idea went from a hobby to a business. For starters, I encourage you to take a self-inventory and find out what you love doing most and are most passionate about. Then allow that to shape what direction your business idea should go in.

Defining Success

You must believe in what you are doing even when others do not.

Next, try to envision what you believe success looks like for you and your new business. A decade ago, individuals were starting companies with an eye on taking them public with a success-at-all-costs attitude. Many of today's entrepreneurs are starting businesses according to an entirely different set of criteria. Take a moment to determine what success means to you. Try answering the following questions:

- What is it that is most important to you at this stage in your life?
- How would you define the success of your business?
- Is your success determined by someone or something else?
- Does success to you translate into a quality-of-life change?

Believe and Focus

Over the years, I have seen friends, family members, and acquaintances let others and the circumstances of life derail their dreams. If you decide to take the business plunge, you must believe in what you are doing even when others don't. Then you must focus that belief into accomplishing your goals.

Thomas Edison described a requisite for success as, "The ability to apply your physical and mental energies to one problem incessantly." Stating that the only difference between his success and that of others was that while others spent their time and energies pursuing a great many things, he spent his time on one thing. "If they applied it in one direction ... they would succeed."

Although these points don't guarantee that your idea will be a raging success, I do believe that if you focus on doing what you love, have a clear idea about what success means to you, believe in what you are doing, and make a focused commitment to get your ideas accomplished, it will then no longer be a matter of *if* your ideas and dreams will take shape—but simply a matter of *when*.

Do What You Love

There are no secrets to small business success, yet most small businesses start off as hobbies. If you haven't already, take the time to evaluate the following questions:

- Do you have any hobbies that could be a good foundation for starting a business?

- If so, describe what are they?

- Over the long run, do you think you would enjoy running your hobby as a business?

3

A Closer Look at Business Plans

I've had a small business for a few years. The company performs a variety of services related to environmental projects. I would ultimately like to expand into alternative fuels as well. I currently don't have a business plan; it's more like a business sketch in my head. Can you point me in the right direction that will help me pull together funding?

Congrats on the vision you have for your company; however, you said something that really caught my attention, "I currently don't have a business plan; it's more like a business sketch in my head." Lynn H. Colwell of the former *Business Start-Up Magazine* said, "Starting a business without a plan is like trying to repair a flat tire with your teeth. It may be possible, but you sure make it hard on yourself."

What Is a Business Plan?
Writing a business plan is equivalent to the old saying, "How do you eat an elephant?. ... One bite at a time." Because this document can be massive, it's important to approach it in this manner in order to not get overwhelmed. It's important to understand that a business plan is a written document that clearly defines the goals of a business

9

and outlines the methods for achieving those goals. A business plan

- describes what a business does;
- how it will be done;
- who has to do it;
- where it will be done;
- why it's being done; and
- when it has to be completed.

I will try to break the process down into four main sections.

Avoiding Ineffective Management

Business plans are supposed to help you avoid the pitfalls of new business development or expansion and, as a result, each section should look to clearly describe how the company will address each of these issues. The first has to do with having a lack of managerial experience. Here are some important plan elements to keep in mind for this section:

- *Executive summary:* Often overlooked in its importance is the executive summary. This section of the plan should be written last because it serves as an abstract of the entire business plan. Imagine that Mr. Money Bags is looking to invest in a hot, new idea. The word gets out that results in his receiving hundreds of business plan ideas every day. When he gets to your business plan, he will likely have time to only glance through your executive summary, if that. Will your executive summary be compelling enough in the first 30 seconds to capture the reader's attention and leave the investor wanting to read more? It should be effective and concise and no more than two pages long.

- *Mission:* I believe that every business has a heart and a soul. What is at the very core of your business? A well-thought-out mission statement will help you to better understand the overall vision of your company. A clearly communicated mission statement should

  - state what business your are really in;
  - determine the guiding principles of the company; and
  - communicate what makes this company unique.

  It's important to remember that you probably won't nail your mission statement on the first try. So don't be afraid to write it, set it down, and then come back to it.

- *Products or services:* Have you ever had someone describe their business to you but you left as confused as you started? I don't want you to be that person, so it is important to clearly describe your company's products or services with an emphasis on anything new you are offering. Is your offering unique and can you easily relay the benefits of what you're proposing?

Greater Marketing ROI

Of all of the changes that small business has seen over the years, the biggest changes have come in marketing. With the explosion of Web 2.0 sites, social networks, and a host of other new media options, the marketing landscape has completely morphed into something almost unrecognizable. I have seen many owners caught off guard and still using archaic forms of marketing, with little or no return on their investment. For the marketing section of the plan, be sure to address the following:

- *Business and industry profile:* Do you have experience working in the industry you are looking to open a business in? If so, now is the perfect time to draw on that experience in writing this section of the plan. If not, this section of the plan is that much more important. What significant trends are taking place in your industry? Is your marketplace growing at a rate large enough to handle an influx of competitors, or is it on the decline? Are there key success factors that your company must tap in to in order to be successful? If you are going to enter into a specific industry, your business plan should demonstrate that you have a commanding knowledge of that industry.

- *Marketing strategy:* The S.W.O.T. Analysis has been around since the beginning of time. If you are going to compete against others more established in the industry, you have got to know what your company's strengths, weaknesses, opportunities, and threats are. Once you have determined how you stack up against your competition, you will have a better idea as to how you should best position yourself in the market.

- *Watch the competition:* I once read an article that discussed how the CEO of one international company would often visit his main competitors' stores and simply walk the aisles to see how they stacked up against the industry leader. So there is nothing wrong with doing a little black ops on the competition. In particular, pay close attention to their marketing and whether it's working. Next, describe what marketing tools you intend to use and how they will help you obtain customers.

Know the Numbers

The financial section is by far the most attractive part of your business plan for investors and should be twice as important for you because it describes how your company plans to make money. This section focuses only on the main financial documents that you should have and lenders or investors will expect you to have.

- *Start-up budget:* This is simply a document that describes how much money you will need to get this new company off the ground. Usually, these costs are categorized as one-time expenses, such as fixtures and equipment, starting inventory, any start-up professional expenses, and licenses or advertising.

- *Balance sheet:* It's important to think of a balance sheet as a snapshot in time of your company's assets and liabilities. On the asset side, this document looks to take into account cash on hand, accounts receivables, inventory, property, and equipment. On the liability side, the document looks to capture accounts payable and other long-term debt.

> *"Starting a business without a plan is like trying to repair a flat tire with your teeth. It may be possible, but you sure make it hard on yourself."*
>
> —*Lynn H. Colwell*

- *Income statements:* One of the simplest documents to wrap your mind around as a new owner—and most fun, if you can call spreadsheets fun— are the profit and loss statements. Usually, these documents cover all revenue-related items, including all products and services offered by the company. In addition, the document looks at all company-related expenses, giving the business owner a month-to-month profit update.

The Keys to a Business Plan

Over the years, I have seen a lot of individuals get overwhelmed by the mere thought of taking on a business plan by themselves. For that reason, I have purposefully omitted certain sections of the business plan. Although there is no recipe for creating a business plan that will ensure small business success, I think the following tips will be helpful. Here are a few items that most plan writers usually omit that I want to bring to light.

- For starters, the key to writing a good business plan comes down to doing quality research at the outset; this research will drive the development of your business plan.

- A lot of first-time business owners and first-time plan writers take their business plan at face value. Don't forget to plan for the unexpected because you know what they say about the best laid plans and Murphy's Law.

- Remember to write a great executive summary because it could be the one thing that gets you an audience with the folks holding the purse strings.

- The first business plan I ever wrote read like the phone book and was as thick as one, so make sure that your plan is specific and realistic.

- Lastly, be sure to use an appendix to complement your business plan, and include all supporting documentation, including research, organizational charts, and résumés.

A well-written business plan could bring you one step closer to find-ing the funding you need and one step closer to achieving your small business goals.

Communicate Your Idea

Along with good research, clarity of any business idea is a good starting place for an effective business plan. Try writing a descriptive paragraph for your new company's product or service. Answering these questions could put you on the right path.

- Does it clearly allow readers to understand what it is that you do?

- What is it about your product or service that is unique compared to your competition?

- How do customers benefit from buying your prod-uct or using your service?

4

Which Incorporation Is Right for You?

Flying Solo

Choosing the proper incorporation for your business is one of the most important decisions you will make in establishing your company. Here are some important points to consider:

- Taxes: You must be aware of taxes because your decision will ultimately determine how much you pay in personal and business taxes.
- *Liability exposure:* You must determine how much personal liability you are willing to assume.
- *Control:* Choosing certain forms of business ownership could mean that you lose some level of control of your company.
- *Cost of formation and administration:* These requirements play a huge role in choosing the right structure because some forms of incorporation and their annual filing requirements are much more costly than others are.

Making a case for each form of incorporation would take more time and paper than what is necessary at this point—although I will give you a shortcut later in this section. My goal right now is to place you on the path of least resistance to business incorporation and to point you in the direction of accompanying documents that you will need from the outset.

A Case for Proprietorship

A sole proprietorship is described as a business owned and operated by one person. According to U.S. Census data, firms incorporated as sole proprietorships account for roughly 72 percent of all business incorporations in the United States. A closer look at sole proprietorships and it's easy to see why it has been the incorporation of choice.

For starters, establishing a proprietorship is the easiest way to get started. You first want to file an *assumed name certificate* with your county clerk's office or state corporation or business division. This is usually a two-page document that asks for the basics such as the business name, address, and owner's information. In most cases, you can expect to pay up to $50 in filing fees. Secondly, you want to make sure that your type of business doesn't require any particular or specialty business license such as a day care center or a bed and breakfast might require. You also want to be aware of types of businesses that local governments will not allow to avoid any future problems. Also, the amount of ongoing paperwork is minimal because proprietors are subject to only a single tax (personal income tax rate) and are required to fill out a form called a *Schedule C (Form 1040) Profit or Loss from Business* and include this figure on their personal income tax Form 1040.

> *Sole proprietors account for roughly 72 percent of all business incorporations in the U.S.*

A Social Security Number for Your Business

Regardless of what form of incorporation you choose, you want to apply for an *Employer Identification Number (EIN)*, Form SS-4.

Think of the EIN as a Social Security number for your business. Because you need a business account separate from your personal finances, most banks won't allow you to open an account without one. This document requires only one page of information to complete, including the type of entity, number of first-year employees expected, and the principal merchandise sold or service provided. Did I mention that the Internal Revenue Service doesn't charge for this service? You can also submit this document via the IRS website, an automated phone system, mail, or fax.

Tax Filing Made Easy

If you go into business for yourself, keeping good records is important. Although plenty of business owners do it themselves, I recommend that small business owners leave the tax filing to the professionals. Currently, my accountant handles all of my taxes. At a minimum, I recommend using a bookkeeper to keep your records together. If you choose to file your own taxes, you will most likely fill out a Schedule C (Form 1040) Profit or Loss from Business. This two-page tax document consists of five main sections, including business income and expense information, any information regarding the cost of goods sold, business vehicle information, and other miscellaneous business expenses. Choosing to incorporate is an important decision that has long-reaching implication for both the business and the owner.

The Good and the Bad

Like any form of business incorporation, proprietorships have their share of drawbacks. As a sole proprietor, the owner and the business are one in the same. This opens the door to this form of business's greatest disadvantage: *unlimited personal liability*. This places the personal assets of the owner at risk for any outstanding debts pursued by a creditor or for any legal claims against the business. Also, unless the owner has a great amount of personal wealth, proprietors can often find it difficult to raise the funds necessary to grow the business. Another drawback is that entrepreneurs, even with adequate help, can still find themselves in over their heads. Sole proprietors by default "'wear all hats," and dividing their energies to address so many different needs could mean that they are often less effective on a day-to-day basis. Whereas corporations (and some partnerships) are designed to be ongoing enterprises, if a sole proprietor is unable to continue operating the business for any reason, the organization could dissolve instantly. With all of these uncertainties, along with the financial constraints, sole proprietors often find recruiting and retaining top talent difficult.

It's important to remember that your ultimate choice of incorporation depends on the overall complexity of your business and the advice you receive from a knowledgeable accountant or attorney. Once your business takes off (and it will), you may find that you have outgrown this form of incorporation, that it no longer suits your needs or your company's needs. If you find that to be the case, you can easily convert to a more suitable business form in the future.

Navigating the Process

Determining the right form of incorporation for your business can be confusing. To help you to navigate the process, download Characteristics of Major Forms of Business Incorporation from The Entrepreneur Café, LLC, website at www.ecafellc.com/resources.

5

Owners Should Exercise Caution When Partnering

Looking to Partner

During the seven years that I lived in Southern Illinois, I had the pleasure of working with the College of Business at John A. Logan College. Each spring I would take what I knew from the business development world into the classroom. One of the more memorable questions from my Small Business Management course came from a student who was strongly considering forming a business partnership with a friend. Previously, we explored what makes sole proprietorships so popular as well as some of their major drawbacks. Often teaming up with a friend or acquaintance sounds like an easy path to success; however, small business partnering is very much misunderstood, and partnering of any kind should be entered into with caution.

Are Partnerships a Recipe for Disaster?

Partnerships can be attractive for several reasons, including ease of formation, increased skill sets, and flexibility. However, many business owners are unaware of the potential pitfalls when considering a partnership. For instance, one partner (referred to as the *general partner*) is exposed to unlimited personal liability for any outstanding debts of the business. Partners are also bound by what is called the law of agency. This means that each partner is an agent of the business and can bind the other partners to contracts—even without their knowledge. Another major problem is that over time, divergent views and directions can begin to interfere with day-to-day business operations causing rifts between the partners or, worse, bringing the business down.

Get an Agreement

If you are seriously considering a partnership, make drafting a partnership agreement your top priority. A *partnership agreement* is a document that states in writing the terms under which the partners agree to operate the business and protect each other's interests. Every business partnership should be based on the items agreed upon by the partners in the agreement. The following are a few of the questions the agreement should address:

- What will each partner's roles be?
- How will company ownership be divided?
- How will major decisions be made?
- What is each partner's vision for the company?
- How will any sale of a partner's interest in the company be handled?

Parting Thoughts on Partnerships

If you find yourself in a partnership that has taken a turn for the worse, keep in mind that a partnership is much like a marriage. Start by trying to get to the real issues bothering you or the other partners—remember, communication is key. Things may not turn around immediately, but the key is to remain open about working toward a resolution, if for no other reason than for the sake of the business. If all else fails, be sure to seek legal advice.

If you think this couldn't happen to you, consider this. After hiring an unemployed buddy in 1997 and giving him a 50 percent share of his inventory-tracking business, Baltimore entrepreneur Jay Steinmetz quickly realized that he had made a mistake. When all was said and done, Steinmetz had been locked out of his own company, spent time in jail as a result of the feud, had his business accounts and inventory liquidated to the tune of more than $134,000, and became the victim of a slander campaign by his former partner. Improper planning cost Jay Steinmetz his original dream.

Each partner can bind the other partners to contracts—even without their knowledge.

My advice is to use partnerships as a last resort and even then exercise extreme caution.

Comparing Incorporation Options

Using the Characteristics of Major Forms of Business Incorporation Table you reviewed in the last chapter, try answering the following questions:

- How much personal liability are you willing to assume?

- How much control over the organization would you like to have or be willing to give up?

- What are your current and future financial needs, including tax and capital needs?

- Based on your answers to these questions, which form of incorporation would be the most beneficial for your organization?

6

Mission Statements Keep Your Business on Course

There is something in the words of a well-written mission statement and a company that goes out of its way to stand behind that mission that truly makes a connection with the consumer. From time to time, we encounter companies that seem to have lost their way, which can be chalked up to a bunch of factors. Given the pace of business today, changing technology trends, and a roller coaster economy, it's easy to understand how a company could get turned around. Those factors aside, I think this lack of business clarity could at times be traced to wavering from the company's mission statement or worse—the lack thereof. If you find that your company has unexpectedly gone off of the beaten path, don't fret. With a little redirection and a focus on shoring up your company's mission statement, you could be back on track in no time.

Why a Mission Statement?

As a rule of thumb, I recommend that every business or organization invest in the time that it takes to build a quality mission statement. A company's mission statement should summarize what the company does and what principles guide its day-to-day activities. A good mission statement should accurately explain why your organization exists and what it hopes to achieve in the future. Your mission statement is an opportunity to define your business at the most basic level. It should tell your company's story, ideals, what you do, what you stand for, and why you do it.

Upon Closer Examination

Take a moment to examine the following mission statement:

The mission of The Walt Disney Company is to be one of the world's leading producers and providers of entertainment and information. Using our portfolio of brands to differentiate our content, services, and consumer products, we seek to develop the most creative, innovative, and profitable entertainment experiences and related products in the world.

> *A mission statement is a dynamic, living, breathing, work in progress.*

- Does the company's mission do anything for you?
- Do you feel that Disney's mission is crafted to make a connection with you on a more personal level?
- What about the company's mission statement works for you?
- Based on your own experiences, do you feel that The Walt Disney Company has done a good job over the years of sticking to its mission of providing quality family entertainment?

Simple Mission Guidelines

As you reexamine your own mission statement, answer the following questions:

- What beliefs and values are expressed about your organization?
- Have you clearly described your firm's products and services?
- What markets do you compete in?
- Does your mission statement clearly explain who your target customers are and their characteristics?
- Can the readers of your mission statement clearly identify what needs and wants your company satisfies?
- Does your mission statement identify your major strengths and what competitive advantage your company holds?

It's important to think of your mission statement as the heart and soul of your company. Your mission statement is a dynamic, living, breathing statement, a work in progress. Be sure to revisit and refine it until it resonates not only with you but also with all who read it.

Mission Possible

Examine the mission statements of the following companies. Using the six guidelines for developing a strong mission statement presented above, how would you rate them? Using those same guidelines, try writing and then rewriting your own mission statement.

- Google: "To organize the world's information and make it universally accessible and useful."

- Harley Davidson: "We fulfill dreams through the experiences of motorcycling, by providing to motorcyclists and to the general public an expanding line of motorcycles, branded products, and services in selected market segments."

- eBay: "eBay's mission is to provide a global trading platform where practically anyone can trade practically anything."

- Apple: "Apple is committed to bringing the best personal computing experience to students, educators, creative professionals, and consumers around the world through its innovative hardware, software, and Internet offerings."

- Starbucks: "To inspire and nurture the human spirit—one person, one cup, and one neighborhood at a time."

7

Give Me an Hour and Some Crayons, and I'll Give You a Business

When it comes to developing a new business idea, or even expanding on company plans, two things are sure to happen. The thought of jumping feet first into a new venture or risking expansion in questionable economic times could scare you to death forcing you to cut short your plans. The other likelihood is that you will rise to the challenge, meeting business uncertainty head-on and seeing your idea through to completion. Regardless of the scenario, I think I have the answer to help start-ups and existing business owners address their most pressing business issues all in the time it takes you to grab lunch.

Go Back to Kindergarten

There are times when working on a project that I reach the point of diminishing returns. When this happens, I find that I end up putting in more energy and getting back little in terms of productivity. For me this means that it's time to go back to kindergarten. Kindergarten conjures up images of playing, coloring, and fun! When pen and paper just won't get it done, it's time to bust out a pack of crayons (or markers if you prefer) and a large sheet of drawing paper to tackle business problems in a new and fun way. For many business owners, the idea of "playing" with their business is unthinkable because the theme of the day is all about keeping their heads above water. With crayons and posterboard-sized paper in hand, the first thing you need to do is determine which company issue is most pressing and needs to be addressed first. Is it a management issue? Are you looking for new ways to market? Is your company just now starting out? Once you make that determination, then you're ready to get started.

Time to Get Creative

Now that you have identified your most pressing issue, start by drawing a picture that represents that issue in the center of the page. Try not to get sidetracked by your drawing ability (or in my case, inability). Once you have drawn your central image, begin drawing any and all images that come to mind that are related to solving your most pressing problem. The images don't have to be sequential or logical as long as you can recognize what you have drawn. After you have gotten all of your images (ideas) drawn on the page, take a moment to write one key word that describes what that image is. These keywords should provide a clear connection to the problem or issue you are trying to solve. Lastly, step back from your masterpiece to prioritize which items need to be addressed first (if at all).

Can you clearly describe your product or service?

Answer the Questions

If you have managed to last this long, then know that you are almost done. But first, you must answer some important questions:

- Looking at your work, can you come up with a name for your company?

- Can you clearly describe your product or service?
- What personnel and staff are needed to help you pull this project off?
- What is the most creative marketing technique that you can think of to help you get your idea noticed?
- How much will it cost to implement these plans?

If you can answer these questions, then the time spent visualizing your business has been well spent.

What's the Goal?

Many of you reading this may be thinking, "I don't have time for games." All I can say is that's too bad. I have been visualizing ideas for more than a decade now, and I can tell you that it's great for accomplishing the following:

- It helps you generate more out-of-the-box ideas in less time.
- It helps you to present tons of information in a small amount of space.
- For those of you who find running your business these days to be a grind, it's just plain fun!

Mapping out your ideas in this manner won't solve all of your problems but should provide some instant insight on how to address some very specific company issues. Hopefully, this exercise will help you develop new product or service ideas and find creative ways to market your company. Finally, use your work to try to make a good estimate of how much it will cost to put your plans into action. Give it a try, and be sure to let me know if any amazing ideas come about as a result.

Mind Mapping Your Way to Success

Some time ago I found an amazing Mind Map of the company Zappos. To gain a better understanding for developing a Mind Map of your own, download the Zappos Mind Map from The Entrepreneur Café, LLC, website at www.ecafellc.com/resources. All mind maps don't need to be as detailed as the one created by Zappos. It should simply convey the majority of your thoughts and ideas visually. Based on your personal interaction with the company, do you think that the ideas created in the Zappos Mind Map have translated well in real life?

8

Resolutions for Small Business Success

At the time that this section was written, the business news was dominated by headlines of a struggling economy, unemployment numbers, and credit crunches. These stories overshadowed the fact the entrepreneurs across the country and throughout the world were finding ways to survive and even thrive during difficult times. As I sit on the verge of a new year, it occurs to me that entrepreneurs are, by their very nature, optimistic. I believe that this glass-half-full attitude and a focus on some key business resolutions can go a long way toward getting the new year started off right.

Focus on Goals

Each year as the holidays roll around, I find myself doing the same thing. I begin to spend a little more time evaluating The Entrepreneur Café, LLC's, business plan and conducting a review of the company's future plans. It ensures that I have enough time to prepare for the upcoming year, and come January 1, I'm ready to go.

I like to encourage owners to choose one time of the year to do a full review of their company's business plan. Juggling the day-to-day operations of a business leaves little time for staying on top of this process on a regular basis. If this sounds like you, then try developing three strong business goals that you believe you can successfully implement over the course of the upcoming year. Let's say that one of your goals for the year is to crack the $250,000 sales barrier. With that goal in mind, try to determine what obstacles might stand in your way and what objectives need to be completed to reach that goal. It's also important to chart your progress throughout the year, revising your plans as necessary.

Get Creative

The level of marketing sophistication has grown by leaps and bounds over the last decade. A recurring question I often hear is, Where can I put my marketing dollars that will provide the most return and exposure for my company? My response is usually to look beyond the conventional marketing options in pursuit of some creative, low-cost to no-cost marketing techniques that truly get your company noticed.

A hallmark of the entrepreneurial community is the ability to generate great ideas quickly.

One of the more memorable pieces of marketing I have seen involved a 24-year-old, unemployed college graduate, David Rowe, who took to the streets of London armed only with a sandwich board over his suit. The sandwich board read, "Job Wanted, History Graduate, Interview Me, Prepared to Work First Month Free." The sign caught the attention of a recruitment firm and landed him a job. Who says marketing has to be costly or complicated to be effective?

Innovate Quickly and Often

A hallmark of the entrepreneurial community is the ability to generate great ideas and then figure out what sticks. But how does one manage the day-to-day operations while bringing fresh ideas to market? Depending on your line of business, try not to let new ideas stray too far from your core business. Be open to allowing others to give your idea some constructive criticism. Try to determine early on if your new idea solves a large enough problem and if there exists a big enough target market to support the company's efforts. Lastly, try to get projects completed and ready to be marketed in less time than expected and under budget. This will ensure that you don't invest too much time and money on a project that may not go far.

It's important to not view these concepts as merely planning points for a new year. Although there is no guaranteed recipe for small business success, by focusing on achieving a few key company goals, getting creative with your marketing, and innovating new ideas quickly, you could be well on your way to a promising year.

Creating Business Resolutions

- Try to determine the biggest obstacle facing your company at the present moment. Is it a management, marketing, or financial issue?

- Write one major goal you would like to achieve related to that area.

- How will you support that goal? Write three concrete objectives that will help you to achieve the desired goal.

9

For Quality Advice, Advisory Boards Can't Be Overlooked

My first credible business venture was the Young Entrepreneurs Program, a nonprofit dedicated to youth entrepreneurship that I started in 1996. At the time, I recognized that I needed a little (make that a lot) of help. So I immediately went out and found those individuals who could help me get things done.

At critical times of the year, I try to assess what has worked over the past year, what hasn't worked, and what's on the horizon for the upcoming year. A recent evaluation revealed that I needed to upgrade my current roster of advisers in some key areas. As an entrepreneur, I find that there are times when I lack the insight or objectivity that it takes to continue to move my business forward. If you are just starting out in business, or feel that your business is in need of some new ideas or fresh energy, now may be a good time to establish an advisory board.

What Is an Advisory Board?

One thing to keep in mind is that an advisory board differs from a board of directors in that a board of directors is a legal entity that has an obligation to the organization that it serves. A board of directors is responsible for the partial or full governing of that organization. An advisory board is more of an informal collective of businessmen and women of varying backgrounds willing to donate their time and energy to helping your company take the next big step. The right advisory board can give your company instant credibility and open doors to greater small business opportunities. Unlike a board of directors, this group has limited power, offering mainly advice on some of your company's most pressing issues versus wielding an iron fist over company decisions.

Advisory Goals

Before you begin your pursuit of advisory board members, try creating a set of guiding principles needed to govern your advisory board. Develop a short list of goals that you would like to see your advisory members address. If you are a growing nonprofit that needs to do some serious fundraising, then your advisory board should be all about raising money. If your organization is looking to expand its Rolodex, then networking might be the theme of your board. Do you feel that your current business insight could use a boost? If so, your board might want to focus on developing new business ideas or gaining perspective on existing products and services. After developing your list of goals, choose your top goal to guide the efforts of your advisory board.

> *The right advisory board can open doors to greater small business opportunities.*

What to Look For

Starting out, I think that advisory boards are best served by professionals with whom you already have some working relationship. Only you know what or whom your organization needs, but I would definitely recommend a money person or someone with accounting, finance, or fundraising experience. I also recommend seeking the advice of an attorney to help you navigate legal issues. If your marketing has grown stagnant, consider bringing on a member better suited to implement marketing in a web 2.0 world. Lastly, if your company needs to make a greater connection with the constituents in the area you serve, consider courting someone with a reputation for strong community leadership to build ties.

Next, write a description of the responsibilities, activities, and authoritative limits for each advisory board member. Determine early on if you plan to offer compensation in the form of providing food and beverages at meetings, covering basic expenses, or providing some sort of cash incentive—although financial compensation isn't always required.

After determining your overall advisory board's goals and identifying the skill set needed from individuals, try generating a list of three to five names that fit the bill. Remember that quality advisers rarely waste time on less than stellar business concepts, so make sure that your ideas are of substance.

Just having an advisory board doesn't automatically ensure success; an entrepreneur must be receptive to the advice given and be willing to work hard to implement that advice. Make sure that you are prepared to address company issues by scheduling to meet with your advisers two to four times a year. Meetings should be no more than two to three hours each and should be documented. Lastly, be sure to focus on a few core strategies at each meeting, and get all agenda items out at least two weeks in advance. Following these guidelines will ensure that you will get the most out of your advisory board.

Developing an Advisory Board

Looking back at my first group of advisors, I realized that I was really lucky. I had a great community organizer and educator, a dynamic attorney, and a solid financial guy. With these dedicated members, I was able to navigate some major business pitfalls as I looked to grow my young organization. The following information should be helpful in creating your own advisory board.

- Determine the overriding goals that you would like your advisory board to address.

- What specific business skills does your organization need in order to help you reach your goals?

- Develop a list of ten qualified individuals that meet your needs as advisory board member. Then reach out to them to see if they would be interested in assisting you.

10

Analysis Is Key to Outwitting the Competition

In the summer of 2006, I watched as Office Depot opened its doors near the mall in Carbondale, Illinois. With a Staples store a few blocks away, I admit I was a bit skeptical. Less than a year and a half later a December 2008 headline read, "Carbondale Office Depot Store Slated to Close." The Carbondale store was one of 112 stores scheduled to close in the United States at the time. I have often wondered what was it about that strategic decision that seemed an obvious no that a major corporation like Office Depot had overlooked. A S.W.O.T. analysis of office supply giant Staples reveals where Office Depot went wrong and offers amazing insight for small businesses.

Building on Your Strengths

One thing that sticks out about Staples is the power of its brand. In surpassing Office Depot as the No. 1 office supplier in 2004, Staples has gone on to build one of the most recognizable brands in the world. Staple's brand is so strong that the company is able to sell these mystical Easy Buttons that do absolutely nothing or at best are glorified paperweights. To build on this brand, the company launched an in-house product and packaging-design department. This is considered unusual for a retailer who would normally contract this work out. To date, the company has won dozens of patents for its design work.

Hard Pressed for Weaknesses

For the most part, we have lived in a more-is-better society. However, as consumer preference continues to shift, big-box retailers have begun downsizing their stores in exchange for shoebox locations a fraction of the size. The question I pose is, How much office supply store does the average consumer really need? By paying attention to the fall in retail sales, Staples was able to create a strategy that allowed it to capitalize on this downward trend. What if Office Depot had beaten Staples to the punch in opening smaller, less expense heavy stores while looking to meet the greater needs of the market online? Instead, Staples found its own Achilles' heel and took action to guard itself by opening smaller stores in urban and suburban areas compared with its initial megastore strategy.

Looking for Opportunities

Several years ago, Staples launched the Invention Quest contest, partnering with inventors worldwide to offer an exclusive line of private-label products. This contest brings tens of thousands of new visitors to the company each year. In 2005, Staples aligned itself with Donald Trump's show *The Apprentice*, where contestants were asked to develop a useful desk organizer. The partnership garnered Staples the equivalent of an hour-long commercial, where the winning product landed on Staples' shelves and was an instant hit, selling out on its first day and bringing the company a huge amount of exposure. Staples has also become the second largest Web retailer behind Amazon.com by offering outstanding customer service while allowing customers to conveniently stock up on all of their favorite office supplies from the comfort of their home or office. Lastly, in pursuit of the next big opportunity, the company has partnered with Automatic Data Processing, Inc., to provide customers with payroll and tax services. It seems as if the company is always looking for the next big opportunity.

What Constitutes a Threat?

Threats can come in different forms and from different directions, but the biggest threat to the office supply industry comes in the form of one word. There is an old saying that goes, "Anything you can do Walmart can do better." With the Web taking greater prominence in practically every industry, it's not unrealistic to think that retail giant Walmart could ask for its share of the $40 billion office supply market. That alone is enough to leave most retailers shaking in their boots and doesn't take into account other online companies looking for market share as well.

Know when to pick a fight and when to turn tail so that you live to fight another day.

I would guess that the quick opening and closing of Office Depot's Carbondale store was not a part of their long-term strategy. The reality is that with so many things stacked in their competitor's favor, why would the company pursue those plans in the first place? We might not have all of the answers, but my hope is that this basic analysis reveals something very important to small business owners. Knowing how you stack up against the competition can help determine when it's time to pick a fight and when it's time to turn tail so that you live to fight another day.

Your S.W.O.T Analysis

A common mistake that many small business owners make is assuming that no competition exists because their company is special or because their idea is unique. The goal of this exercise is to determine your company's strengths, weaknesses, opportunities, and threats as they relate to your company and uncover any hidden competition and what competitive advantages they hold in the industry. Download the S.W.O.T. Analysis Table from The Entrepreneur Café, LLC, website at www.ecafellc.com/resources for help with completing this exercise.

11

Operating a Business on the Cheap

One of my favorite small business topics would have to be the idea of running your small business for little or next to nothing. With access to capital shrinking, many small business owners (out of necessity) are forced to learn how to make a very little go a long way. For even the most basic of small business ideas, when factoring in IT needs, inventory, and licenses—among other things—start-up costs alone could put you out $7,000 to $10,000. And that's before you have conducted one month of business. With more companies leveraging new technology, entrepreneurs have learned how to operate their businesses more cost effectively than many of their larger counterparts. Running a small business is never easy, but my hope is that the following information will provide a few tips for holding on to more of your hard-earned money while growing your business.

Learn to Coexist

For years, entrepreneurs and professionals have been abandoning their traditional offices for the cost savings and flexibility of shared office space, known as coworking. One of the ways clients benefit from coworking is by sharing customers. Cowork tenants also share office equipment such as copy/fax machines as well as break and conference rooms. Coworking also benefits tenants by providing greater networking opportunities and can save an owner as much as $300 to $400 a month in utility costs alone.

If coworking is still out of reach, try turning that spare bedroom or oversized closet into your dream office. This could ultimately limit the types of business that can be conducted at this location and could limit your meeting schedule as you become a bit more selective of whom you allow to meet at your home office. However, this move could save your company from $500 to $1,000 over a traditional office or coworking.

Recycle Office Equipment

A while back, a friend stopped by my office with a couple of computers to donate after his office had upgraded equipment. From time to time, established businesses might upgrade computers, software, or both. If you play your cards right, you could find that some of these companies might be interested in parting with these slightly used machines, depending on how compelling you are. Ask around to see if there are any companies in your area that might be upgrading equipment soon and then follow up. Another option is to check out Craigslist (www.craigslist.com), which allows you to search your local area for free or nominally priced equipment to serve your needs until you get on your feet. While searching for items on your equipment list, be sure to browse the site for all of your office furniture needs as well. I guarantee that with a little research, you will be able to meet all of your equipment and furniture needs and save a ton of money in the process.

Entrepreneurs have learned to operate their businesses more efficiently than many of their larger counterparts.

Cancel Your Travel Plans

We're all at the mercy of the gas pump. As prices continue to climb, the following ideas could be the key to cutting travel expenses.

If it doesn't pose too much of an inconvenience, try using public transportation to connect for business in your local area. I recently moved to an area that has one of the best transportation systems in the country, and I'm using my car less and less. You will easily find savings in gas, parking, and fender benders all while someone else does the driving for you.

With so many new technologies to choose from, I encourage you to evaluate whether it would be possible to substitute some of your face-to-face meetings with the convenience of a conference call. Teleconference technology leaders Skype (www.skype.com) and ooVoo (www.ooVoo.com) make it easy to connect face to face with anyone across town or around the world. I have at least one teleconference call a week, which allows me to get some quality work done while not moving a muscle.

Ideas for Cutting Small Business Expenses

I am constantly looking for ways to operate my business more cost effectively. I hope that the following ideas will offer some insight for how you can do the same.

- If coworking and working from home are non options, try locating three places that you can go to get some solid work done at critical times. Book a meeting room at the local library, find a favorite coffee shop, or locate a community center to serve as your temporary office.

- Instead of tossing used folders, try reusing them for another purpose. Can slightly used paper be used as scrap for capturing ideas?

- Determine your biggest office needs and then try to find a free workaround for meeting that need.

- Agree to meet for business over coffee instead of lunch or dinner.

- Automate as many of your company's routine functions as possible.

- Change some of your traditional mailings to include more e-mails, electronic newsletters, and online catalogs.

12

Sparking Small Business Creativity

A study by Yankelovich Partners—a social and marketing research firm headquartered in Chapel Hill, North Carolina—reported that entrepreneurs spend their time in the following ways:

- Administrative tasks, 31 percent of their time
- Financial issues, 30 percent
- Managing employees, 23 percent
- Selling to customers, 28 percent
- Negotiating with suppliers, 23 percent

These same entrepreneurs spend only 38 percent of their time getting actual work done. Ask an overworked business owner how much time she spends fostering new ideas and you are likely to get laughed out of her place of business—or worse. With new ideas representing possible new avenues of growth, how can small business owners continue the daily juggling while sparking creativity in their own firms?

Look Past the Paradigms

Most owners can pinpoint the one or two business obstacles standing between them and greater success. In creatively addressing those issues, entrepreneurs must first avoid paradigms. *Paradigms* are preconceived ideas about what the world is, what it should be like, and how it should operate. Before Netflix broke through the video-rental paradigm, most of us couldn't conceive of renting our videos from anywhere but our local Blockbuster Video. In looking for creative solutions for your own company, understand that there is always more than one right answer. The biggest success stories have been written by men and women who chose not to do things by the book. By avoiding being too practical and not always playing it safe, these individuals have been able to avoid paradigms on their way to success.

Can business owners continue their daily juggling while sparking creativity in their own firms?

Becoming a Creative Thinker

Sparking creativity in your company need not be difficult, but dedicating time to this task will take some getting used to. For starters, try developing an idea file. Some of the best ideas come at the most inopportune times, so be sure to write those thoughts down (in the moment) and drop them in the file. Be sure to make time to get back to them later. Always be willing to ask the question, Is there a better way to do this? Don't be afraid to challenge custom, routine, and tradition in thinking through new ideas. As children in school, we are taught to pay attention and not daydream—focus, focus, focus. However, as a business owner, you must take time to be reflective on the outlook of your business. Lastly, it's important to view mistakes and failures as stepping-stones to success and problems as springboards to a whole new world of idea possibilities.

Remember that idea creation doesn't mean much if you are unable to apply those creative ideas and solutions to real problems that enhance people's lives. Millions of individuals have come up with some amazing ideas for different products or services; unfortunately, that is where it ended. The goal should be to see these new ideas through to fruition—it is only then that a company begins to become innovative.

Honing Your Creativity

The list of things that you can do to spark small business creativity is endless. The following is my list for keeping the creative juices flowing.

- Do things that take you out of your comfort zone. When I find things getting stale, I like to mix it up.

- Keep a small notebook handy to capture those fleeting ideas and from time to time review it.

- Get some exercise regularly; it's a great way to clear your head and get refreshed.

- Try being more spontaneous in your plans. A little less structure forces you to think on your feet.

- Take time out to listen to some music or try playing an instrument. The mere act of trying to play an instrument makes you feel more creative.

- Go back and try working on your Mind Map.

- If you have young kids in your family, try playing games with them or working on an art project. I am amazed at how the creativity of my two young sons rubs off on me when we're having fun.

- Get in over your head. Usually when you are working on something that is a stretch for you, it forces you to be creative in figuring out a solution.

- Stay away from distractions; they are creativity killers.

13

Crafting a Confidentiality Agreement

Entrepreneurs are often charged with doing the impossible in order to keep their companies moving forward. What do you do when you find yourself with more projects to complete than available hands or hours in the day? An increasing number of small business owners have turned to freelancers to stay ahead of their workloads. The keys to the successful completion of any freelance project lies in the details of a confidentiality (nondisclosure) agreement. A good confidentiality agreement doesn't have to be wordy or complex or filled with legalese; however, it should spell out the details of the project and protect your company's intellectual property and other sensitive information. My hope is that the following information will serve as a guide for creating your own project-specific confidentiality agreement.

Explain the Purpose

Over the years, I have learned the painful lesson of not assuming that others know what I am talking about. This same rule has served me equally well in the business world as I now make it a priority to explain all new projects in great detail for the benefit of the freelancer and for The Entrepreneur Café, LLC. I often find myself being stretched by some of my new projects in terms of available time. The difference is I now understand the value of asking for help. One of the problems I see all too often is the skepticism of many entrepreneurs to venture out with freelancers for fear of divulging too much information and having their ideas "borrowed."

To be clear about what is expected on both sides, start by describing the *scope of the work*, what the freelancer is responsible for, and a timetable for *deliverable items*. Remember to explain the *duration* of the project, which gives an estimate of the time it will take for the project to be completed and how long the confidentiality agreement is in place for. Lastly, be sure to outline the terms of *compensation* and how and when those payments are to be made.

Be Clear About Confidentiality

When crafting a document to protect your company's intellectual property, describe what you mean by *confidentiality* because it could mean something entirely different to someone else. Be sure to include the term *no use*, which states that the recipient agrees not to use the confidential information in any way except as described in the agreement. Make sure that the recipient understands his obligations in terms of keeping information related to the project safe. A *no disclosure* statement ensures that the recipient agrees to use his best efforts to prevent and protect any part of the project from falling into the public domain and that company ideas of any kind are not to be shared. A statement outlining potential damages expected due to harm caused by an information leak can go a long way in helping your company avoid some potential headaches.

Increasingly, owners have turned to freelancers to stay ahead of their workloads.

No Transfer

Lastly, it is important that the recipient of the information know that his participation in the project does not entitle him to nor imply any transferable rights to the use of any of the information disclosed. Make sure that you note that at the completion of the project, the confidential information shall remain the sole property of you or your company (*discloser*). As a final measure, state in clear language that no copies of the project are to be kept in either printed hard copy or digital form for any personal and professional use. This should help bring clarity to who owns what and the roles of each party. A good nondisclosure agreement can be drafted in a couple of hours and will go a long way in helping get some much needed work off of your desk and provide protection for your company at the same time.

Drafting Your Own Confidentiality Agreement

Download a copy of our Confidentiality Agreement from The Entrepreneur Café, LLC, website at www.ecafellc.com/resources. Feel free to edit this document by adding information that is specific to your company. If you have a legal adviser, now would be a good time to ask for their input on ways to improve this document.

Making Policy Manuals Work for Your Small Business

Last month I packed a bag, grabbed a menacing-looking folder sitting in my file cabinet, and set out for an undisclosed location for a weekend of work. As The Entrepreneur Café, LLC, has grown, it has always been my intention to develop a formal policy manual—one that would be the envy of small businesses everywhere. However, it did not take long before I realized that I was in over my head. My goal was to turn this process from what some view as a scary encounter with human resources into a document that will rally employees and help drive small business growth.

Seeing the Big Picture

At the outset, I wanted to create policies and procedures that would serve as a powerful tool for recruiting and boosting company morale. So I bounced ideas off of advisory board members, contractors, interns, friends, and family in search of one very important answer: Is the culture of The Entrepreneur Café, LLC, one that other individuals can buy in to? I wanted to know if our style of business (how we operate) is respectful of employees', interns', and contractors' personal and professional lives. Long story short, I wanted to create a policy manual that would accurately portray The Entrepreneur Café,

LLC, as a progressive company, one that future employees would want to work for.

Covering the Legal Bases

In creating a policy manual, one thing stood out was the the relationship between a company and its contractors. This is different from the relationship between a company's full and part-time employees. This one issue is goverend by more laws than I realized. The three categories that seemed to warrant the most attention and could cause the most future problems are:

- *Harassment and discrimination:* It is important that companies affirm their commitment as equal opportunity employers in every respect. We are also looking to make plain that the company will not tolerate harassment or illegal discrimination and is trying to outline the steps and processes for handling any potential violations.

- *Wage and hour issues:* This section of a policy manual should look to address the days and hours of the workweek as well as the rules that govern the workday. It should also look to establish clearer guidelines for categorizing employees.

- *Safety:* Work hazards will be less of a daily concern for a service-based company like ours versus, say, a manufacturing company. However, I will have to address any potentially dangerous work-related issues to be in accord with state and federal regulations.

The previous points don't even scratch the surface of what it takes to put together a policy manual but stand out as some of the more pressing issues. For those looking to undertake this task, it's important to know that a policy manual is not for the faint of heart. The sheer amount of internal and external documentation needed could seem endless. As I began working my way through my own policy manual, it became very clear why an entire human resources and workforce development industry exist to handle nothing but these types of issues. No matter how detailed you decide to make your policy manual, it's important to make sure that employees sign off on the fact that they have received and read the handbook, and that they will seek clarification on any aspect of the document that may be unclear. Being thorough in this process could go a long way in meeting the needs of your staff and in building the kind of company culture that many would want to be a part of.

> *My goal was to create a policy manual that would rally employees and drive small business growth.*

Your Policy Manual

It's never too early to begin thinking ahead. As your organization begins to grow, it becomes increasingly important to establish a set of policies that will guide how you manage personnel. This list is not exhaustive but will help in developing your own policy manual.

- How are personnel needs determined? How will the announcement of the new job be handled, and how will the hiring process be conducted?

- Is there a clearly spelled-out job description for new employees, including any current and future job responsibilities, pay, and who the employee reports to?

- To help reduce turnover, how will new hires be oriented to the company and trained?

- How and when will employees be evaluated in their roles, and what are the standards of performance?

- Given the legal climate, companies must protect themselves by establishing a set of practices for how employees who are not working out will be dismissed.

15

Maneuvering Small Business Manufacturing

I have a product that I am trying to bring to market, and I'm having an extremely hard time trying to locate a manufacturer. Do you have any idea how I can find manufacturers capable of producing thin sheets of pliable plastic that can be stamp-cut with adhesive on the opposite side?

I remember getting this e-mail from an inventor in Illinois near the St. Louis area. It had been a while since I had focused my efforts on manufacturing. It immediately took me back to an incident years ago when my wife and I were entertaining thoughts of manufacturing our own line of infant products. As new parents, we were constantly coming up with a better mousetrap (mainly in our minds) or looking for ways to improve on existing child-specific products. In this particular instance, we looked for a product that would keep us from cleaning up breakfast, lunch, and dinner after my son would toss his unwanted food on the floor. We were certain there wasn't anything on the market like it, and so we set out to revolutionize the infant bowl market. It seems that Walmart had the same idea because while we were dragging our feet on the idea, the giant retailer was making it a reality. Although our idea never made it to market, what we learned from that experience was invaluable. The following are some important points to consider when looking to work with a manufacturer.

Know the Patent Process

A patent on your invention grants you property rights to use that product for a period of 20 years and excludes others from making, using, offering for sale, selling, or importing your idea. Be sure to check out the United States Patent and Trademark Office's (USPTO) website (www. uspto.gov). Click on the patent link to learn more about *utility patents* awarded to new and useful processes, machines, composition of matter, or any variation thereof. Unless you are familiar with the details of patent filing, I recommend conducting a patent attorney search to assist you or allowing the USPTO to assign one to your application. Also be prepared to handle multiple application revisions as well as a determination notice of six months or more.

The more versatile your product the greater its chances for success.

I had an opportunity to speak with Jeff Stevens, a former manufacturing specialist with the Illinois Manufacturing Extension Center. According to Jeff, "When considering a supplier for a product or service, there are many important requirements to consider that ultimately determine a customer's satisfaction level. Three of the more important requirements are quality, cost, and delivery."

Quality

Quality is more than just meeting a customer's requirements or specifications. When considering a supplier, internal quality is just as important as external quality. For example, a supplier can produce a product or service that has zero external customer defects. However, if that supplier has poor internal quality (high defect rates, rework, and scrap), the supplier must recoup its cost of that poor quality or go out of business.

Cost

The cost of poor internal quality usually translates into higher costs for the customer. The "extra cost" results in overpriced products or services and higher customer dissatisfaction. These extra costs can take the form of employee absenteeism, safety and litigation issues, design changes, product obsolescence, inventory, long set-up times, and other inefficient uses of human and natural resources. All of these contributors negatively affect the supplier and contribute to extra cost that might ultimately have to be recouped by the customer. So be sure to do your due diligence and choose your manufacturer wisely.

Delivery

Also known as *lead time*, this is the amount of time consumed from ordering raw materials or services to the time that a product or service is delivered to the customer. Long set-up times, excess movement of raw materials, work in process, and scheduling can dramatically affect lead times. So investigate to make sure that you can expect your order as stated.

Don't go into this process blind. Make sure that you get honest feedback on your idea from others not directly involved in the process, and make sure that you take their advice to heart. Find someone that has experience in navigating the process, and ask for that person's advice as well. For more information on finding the right manufacturer for you, a great resource to start with would be the Illinois Manufacturing Extension Center (www.imec.org), 1501 W. Bradley Avenue Peoria, IL 61625 / 1-888-806-4632 / Fax: 309-677-3289 / Email: info@imec.org.

Evaluating Your Manufacturing Strategy

Try finding ways to expand your product or service strategy before bringing it to market in an effort to improve its chances for success.

- Are there cheaper, easier-to-access alternatives already in existence?

- Long term, will you continue to use a supplier or are you interested in owning the manufacturing process?

- How will your product be packaged and who will handle it?

- Will you sell directly to consumers or manufacturers, or will you license your product?

- Are there any secondary applications of your invention? Again, the more versatile your product the greater its chances for success.

16

Business Owners Should Be Prepared to Defend Themselves

I recently came across an article that described how the owners of Internet darling Twitter are engaged in an ongoing fight over trademark rights to the word *Tweet*. A word which is at the very core of their company they don't even own. If you were to poll a handful of business owners, many might admit to giving little thought to the details of protecting their company's intellectual property. Stories abound of companies like Priceline, Twitter, Microsoft, Google, and other big names embroiled in copyright, patent, and trademark infringement cases. If Fortune 500 companies can't escape the legal mire of intellectual property disputes, do small businesses stand a chance? There are multiple ways companies can protect themselves, including patents and copyrights. However, if you have labored to build a company that has a recognizable name, logo, or tagline, it's definitely worth protecting by pursuing a trademark.

What Is a Trademark?
The United States Patent and Trademark Office (USPTO) is in Alexandria, Virginia. If you have ever attempted to navigate the agency's

massive website (www.uspto.gov), you might find yourself quickly in over your head. Before getting started, it's important to understand what a trademark is. *Trademarks are words, phrases, symbols, designs, or combinations thereof that identify and distinguish the source of the goods or services of one party from those of others.* It's important to note that you don't need to obtain a trademark from the USPTO if you have been using your respective mark in commerce for years. Then why take that extra step?

- To serve public notice of your claim to the mark
- To have the entitlement to bring an action concerning the mark in federal court
- To acquire the right to use the registered trademark symbol ®

From personal experience, it's not necessary to hire an attorney unless you are dealing with a complex intellectual property case. If you have an eye for instruction and a little patience, you should be able to navigate the process just fine.

Know What You Want to Protect

Before beginning the application process, know exactly what you want to protect. Are you protecting a *standard character drawing* or a mark consisting primarily of *words, letters,* or *numbers*? If so, think about recognizably trademarked names such as Red Bull, Skype, Twitter, and Google. Burger King, in its effort to be the anti-McDonalds, trademarked "Have it your way." BMW trademarked the claim to building "The ultimate driving machine." And Nike has laid claim to mobilizing a nation of athletes with "Just do it." Steve Jobs knew he was on to something with his forbidden fruit logo, which, absent any color, would be considered an *actual drawing* of the mark. And Coca-Cola, with its scripted name and red-and-white color scheme, is classified as a *special form drawing*, which takes into account the drawing in a particular style of lettering, along with special colors. Once you have classified what you want to protect, you are ready to start the application process.

Be Thorough and Be Patient

There are several ways to file for a company mark. The cheapest and least bureaucratic way is to file online using the *Trademark Electronic Application System*, which could save you about $100. Each trademark application must have a class of goods and services associated with the mark. Classifications span everything from Class 4 Lubricants and Fuels to a Class 41 Education and Entertainment. Avoid choosing too many categories; this could be a quick way to get your application booted. Lastly, don't assume that because you have gone through the painstaking process of submitting the application that it's a done deal—because it's not. If all goes well and there are no objections, you might be able to see a turnaround of 12 weeks, although I've heard of cases taking well over a year. Be prepared to stay on top of the process to make sure that things run as smoothly as possible.

> *A trademark could reduce the likelihood of your company getting confused in the marketplace.*

I don't know many small businesses that can afford the time and expense of getting "lawyered-up" in an effort to protect their company's intellectual property. Investing time in securing a trademark could reduce the likelihood of your company getting confused in the marketplace and reduces the chances of someone reaping the benefits of your hard work. If you have an official trademark and a problem arises, the solution could be as simple as a cease-and-desist letter.

Getting Comfortable with Trademarks

The trademark process, though less intense than submitting a patent, can still be a little intimidating for some. The following should serve as an introduction to trademarks.

- Take some time getting familiar with The United States Patent and Trademark Office's (USPTO) website (www.uspto.gov).

- From the USPTO's homepage, click on the Trademark section and then locate the section entitled Manuals, Guides, and Official Gazette to gain a better understanding of the Trademark process.

- Use the USPTO's Trademark Electronic Search System (TESS) to conduct an initial search of your future word or design-related trademark.

17

Can Southern Illinois Become the Napa Valley of the Midwest?

This topic was one of my favorites. Growing up in Chicago, a person gains a very blue-collar view of how small business is done. Later on living in the Washington, D.C., area I was able to see the convergence of technology, small business, and politics on the small business segment. At the time of this article, I had been in Southern Illinois for almost seven years. During that time, I gained a unique perspective of how areas that look exactly the same across the country are looking to redefine themselves after decades of an economy based on manufacturing, mining, and those that have only a couple of major institutions anchoring them down. How does rural America survive in a web 2.0 world? Here was my take on a recent trip to the beautiful Napa Valley.

For years, I had come across articles, books, and countless movie scenes depicting the sights and sounds of California's magnificent Wine Country. With much urging from my wife, I decided to set work aside to attend a wedding with her in nearby St. Helena so that I could see for myself. If I had to summarize the splendor of this Memorial Day getaway, I would best describe Napa Valley and Sonoma County as a well-oiled machine of tourism with no sign of letting up. Southern Illinois has an ever-growing list of quality wineries, so upon my return, I couldn't help but wonder ... could Southern Illinois become the Napa Valley of the Midwest?

Creating a Scene

The drive from San Francisco to Napa was filled with images of rolling hills, beautiful sunshine, quaint inns, restaurants, and wineries with their acres of grapes. En route to our bed & breakfast, we passed an amazing group of upscale shops spanning everything from art galleries to home decor. This was accompanied by the collective of small fruit stands that dotted the road where local growers were selling their fresh harvest. There was the school of culinary arts, other restaurants, antique shops, and hosts of other businesses that all understood the importance that their roles play in helping one another and for the greater good of Napa and Sonoma. The wineries may headline the area, but the best supporting roles go to those businesses that work together to create one amazing experience.

Southern Illinois has a lot going for it, including its access to neighboring state tourism, the rise of in-state vacationing, scenic drives, top-notch wineries, and people who want to see the region live up to its potential. What's missing are more of the supporting casts businesses, a few huge tourist attractions, and possibly a unified brand that speaks for all of Southern Illinois, like the destination feel that has been created for all of Route 66.

Raise Expectations

One thing that stood out about our Wine Country excursion was that every interaction came with the five-star treatment. The young woman at the San Francisco Office of Tourism was the most knowledgeable tourism professional that I have ever encountered. At Beringer Vineyards, our tour guide (John) had been giving tours for more than ten years. As he discussed the history of wine making in Napa, the winery's founders, the wine-making process, and all things in between, it became very clear that this was not just a job for him. John was passionate about what he did, and that passion translated into a very memorable experience for us. Wine specialist Spencer, at Dean & Deluca, took considerable time in helping us pair our new wines with their never-ending selection of meats and cheeses. Lastly, Chris, who managed our bed & breakfast, made sure that we didn't want for anything over the course of our three-day stay. When all was said and done, everything that I thought I knew about fine dining, good wine, and unique cheeses had all been erased. I found that the Napa Valley had educated me on what makes this region special and, in the process, raised my level of expectation. The whole experience made me wonder how Southern Illinois could leave its visitors wanting more.

How does rural America survive in a web 2.0 world?

Opportunities Abound

I bring up the former points only to say that if you have been thinking of a business idea—especially one that piggybacks on or complements area tourism—then there is no time like the present. Whether you are an entrepreneur looking for your next big opportunity or an entrepreneur-in-training living in a rural region like Southern Illinois or someplace similar, here is my take on some ideas that might go over well. I won't do much to expand on these ideas; I'll leave that up to you. But I encourage you to take these suggestions as just that—mere suggestions.

- *Garden-fresh dining:* Yes, restaurants are the riskiest of ventures, but what if it created a totally different experience? An establishment set right in the place where their fruit and vegetables are grown with meat, poultry, and fish all brought in locally?

- *Customized wine/history tours:* What if a tour operator provided customized wine or history tours catered to the unique interest of an individual, family, or small group?

- *Create a sampler:* Could the various wineries create a sampler of red, white, and dessert wines that would showcase the best that the Southern Illinois' wine trail has to offer.

- *Entertain me:* Adults and kids need more things to do in the area, so how about a great miniature golf experience, a building packed with inflatables, or a hot air balloon ride? My point is that if it's truly entertaining, it just might have a chance.

Transforming the region into a Midwest destination of Napa's magnitude doesn't happen overnight, but with a lot of like-minded entrepreneurs moving in the same direction, you never know what could happen.

Transforming Areas with Big Business Ideas

If you live in a rural area or are looking for a way to contribute to the economic development of your community, the following exercise could help you create new opportunities.

- When was the last time you came across a business idea and wondered if that concept would do well back home?

- What about that idea made it special enough for you to want to try it in your area?

- What is the biggest hindrance to seeing this idea come to life? Is the idea too complicated, does it require more time and energy than you currently have to contribute, or is it cost prohibitive?

18

The Art of Business Networking

I have always found the statistics describing those individuals who would prefer death over public speaking interesting, to say the least. Given the choice, I would choose the latter—at least I could recover from a bad speaking engagement. There is also a growing group that places networking in the same light. Although I can sympathize with those who find working a room of hundreds uncomfortable, I would be remiss if I didn't say that business networking is a necessity. Often the connections we make at these networking events today can lead to business opportunities tomorrow. The key to pulling off a successful networking event is to remember that effective networking is an art.

Be Selective
In the past, I would try to make as many business events as possible. Today, there is more of a method to my madness. Choosing the event that is most appropriate for you and your business is key. As small businesses usually cycle through stages and are dealing with a particular obstacle at different times in this cycle, consider choosing an event that will help address the most pressing need at that time. For instance, if your small business is in phase one of a new website

redesign, try finding a business event that brings together some of the great minds in Web development.

Make the Right Connections

Some of the best business events that I have attended were not only specific to my business's needs but also came with a list of attendees. Having an attendee list allows you to identify individuals and companies of interest before the event. If you are lucky enough to get an attendee list, be sure to do your homework so that when an opportunity presents itself, you will be ready. If you happen to find that one individual whom you are eager to talk to and that person is in a conversation, be patient. Wait until the conversation opens up to you or until the conversation has concluded, and then strike up a conversation of your own.

> *The connections we make today can lead to business opportunities tomorrow.*

Networking Reminders

One of the most important things you can do in preparing for an upcoming business event is to make sure that you have plenty of business cards. You will always wind up exchanging more cards than you think, and there is nothing worse than running out of cards at the most inopportune time. Unless the event is a breakfast, lunch, or dinner networking event, I suggest eating before arriving to the event. This helps you avoid awkward food-in-the-teeth looks or messy handshakes. Be realistic about what you hope to accomplish at these events. Once you have connected with the individuals you have come to meet and have gotten the information you desire, this would be a good time to leave. Lastly, be sure to follow up with the contacts you have made within a week of the event.

The Art of Business Networking

I often take a genuine interest in the business ideas and dreams of other business owners. As a result this makes networking one of my favorite small business activities. Here are some tips for a successful networking event.

- Brush up on your elevator speech, which is a strong description of your company (what you do and how you do it) delivered in about 30 seconds. The easier it is for you to deliver that line, the better your event will go.

- Most areas have enough events to keep even the most avid networker busy; the key is choosing the right one. Find an event that might work for you, and then go try it out. If you find that it's not a good fit, no worries—you are not committed to it and can simply move on to the next one.

- If time restrictions or mere discomfort still keep you from the traditional networking scene, try online social networking sites like LinkedIn (www.linkedin.com). The site has become a preferred method among executives, recruiters, and small businesses looking to connect with one another.

19

Public Relations Done Right

I remember my first real attempt at public relations (PR). I was in college operating as a novice entrepreneur, and my new nonprofit, the Young Entrepreneurs Program (YEP), was just really getting off of the ground. At the time, my strategy was simple: get an envelope, include an archaic brochure with a Post-it note, and then close my eyes, cross my fingers, and hope for the best. The result was that renowned marketer Jerry Fisher wrote an article on the YEP titled "Fishing for Ideas." The article ran in the February 1999 issue of *Entrepreneur Magazine* and brought me a level of national recognition and credibility that would have taken years on my own. Today's public relations efforts are far more sophisticated than my wing-and-a-prayer approach, and when done right, could pay big dividends.

PR 101
Two adages of public relations:

1. If you don't tell your story, then someone else will definitely tell it for you.
2. All PR (even bad PR) is still good PR.

I am a fan of the former, and I think that companies like BP would agree with me. Public relations allows you to connect with the greater viewing audience to let them know what your business is all about. Publicity is not a one-sided deal but a free exchange between you and the media. If you are planning to embark on a public relations campaign, be sure to define your goals and objectives before you begin.

Tips for Getting Started

If managed properly, public relations leads to increased credibility and sales. These tips, although not exhaustive, will definitely start your press efforts off right.

- First, determine if your message is newsworthy. Does your story piggyback on a popular news trend?
- Be selective where you publicize, and determine if the media of choice gives you greater access to your target market.
- Know who covers what, and be respectful of the media's time and deadlines. I often marvel at how reporters and journalists manage to keep it all together.
- Develop a one-page press release with all of the key information front-loaded. Your release should answer who, what, when, where, why, and how.
- Lastly, be sure to check your information for spelling and grammatical errors.

Is your message newsworthy and does it piggyback on a popular story?

Don't confuse public relations with marketing, although it plays a key role in getting your company's message out. In today's hyperconnected society, not all news about your company will leave the general public with warm and fuzzy feelings. Taco Bell

CEO Greg Creed used public relations in defense of a lawsuit that claimed his company was engaging in false advertising. Taco Bell used PR to tell its story and got it right. If you're not using public relations on a regular basis, now is a good time to start.

Developing a Press Strategy

Developing a proper media strategy for your company takes time. The following information will help you become more familiar with the process.

- Try locating a story on a company in your immediate area. What kind of an impression does the article leave you with regarding the company and the owner?

- If you are just starting your business, what's the one thing you would like to tell the world about your new venture? If you have been in business for a while, do you have any newsworthy events coming up in the next three to six months that you would like to publicize?

- Having trouble writing your press release? Download a copy of our Press Release Template from The Entrepreneur Café, LLC, website at www.ecafellc.com/resources and get started crafting your company's media message.

20

To Get Good at Advertising, Know the Formula

Recently, The Entrepreneur Café, LLC, released our newest product, a small business database with hundreds of resources to address small business concerns. Excited that the project was completed, I turned my attention to developing an ad that would effectively communicate exactly what we wanted to say. After finishing a couple of drafts of the ad, I quickly realized that something was missing. Over the years, I have used some variation of this formula; however, I knew that if I wanted to nail this ad, I would have to fall back on what I learned in Advertising 101. If you find yourself struggling with an ad of your own, try using the **A.I.D.A.** formula for an advertising breakthrough.

Do I Have Your Attention?

We are bombarded by hundreds (if not thousands) of advertisements on a daily basis, many of which we are not even aware of. I admit that I have become desensitized to most advertising and notice only those ads with enough bang to get through the clutter. The first A in creating a powerful ad is all about capturing the reader's **Attention.** Six months after the September 11 terrorist attacks, technology company Siebel Systems ran an ad linked to the rollout of its new Homeland Security software. Siebel's attention-grabbing headline read, "Who are the Mohamed Attas of tomorrow?" and included an image of Atta passing through an airport one day before the attacks. I remember that ad as vividly today as when it ran in 2001. If you don't get the attention of your readers immediately, you may have lost them for good.

Can You Build Interest?

So you managed to do the impossible and grab the reader's attention. Now it's time to keep the momentum going, and you do so by building **Interest**. In creating my most recent ad, I tried putting myself in the shoes of my audience when asking, What's in it for me? In thinking my ideas through in this manner, and by getting some great feedback, I realized purchasers of our small business database could expect the following:

- A resource to help business owners generate new ideas
- A database to help entrepreneurs network and share resources with one another
- A database to help owners address management, marketing, and financial concerns

In short, we looked at some of the benefits of our database and tried to present them in a way that created interest for our product.

You're Sunk Without Desire

At this point, you should start to see that each element in our A.I.D.A. formula builds on the other. With that said, the third step is all about creating **Desire**. The way you create desire is by making an emotional connection in the hearts and minds of your audience.

In this section of the ad, your goal is to make sure that your readers are one step closer to buying what you are selling. Interest allows you to clearly spell out the benefits, and desire allows you to offer customers what they can't live without. If you are able to figure that out and communicate it effectively, you are three-quarters of the way to getting the sale.

Time for Some Action

So far so good, as you have managed to capture the reader's attention, build interest in your product or service, and stoke a desire to buy. But you're not done yet. Many advertisers have successfully done the first three only to fail to ask the customer for the business and ultimately lose the sale. The **Call to Action** is key because your customers could be on board up to that point; but if you don't ask, they won't buy. Remember

Capture a reader's attention quickly or you may have lost them for good.

that you can do everything else right but don't forget to give them a reason to pull the trigger. The following are some common calls to action that I have come across over the years:

- For a limited time only, so call today!
- Order now, and as a bonus, we will give you a second set free, but only if you order now!
- If you call within the next 10 minutes, you can save 50 percent off of the original price!

These calls to action may be corny, but these or some variation thereof have been proven to work. Remembering the formula is important, and if you are going to write your own ad, try doing so as if you were looking to connect with one person. If you can connect with one person, then the likelihood that your ad will connect with the masses is greatly improved. Create at least two versions of your ad so that you can measure what works and what does not. Lastly, be open to some quality feedback before you decide to take your ad live.

Putting A.I.D.A. into Action

Download a copy of our A.I.D.A. Matrix from The Entrepreneur Café, LLC, website at www.ecafellc.com/resources for insight on how we created one of our recent ads. Use the matrix to complete the exercise below in creating your own advertisement.

- Try drafting several short Attention-grabbing titles and subtitles.

- Try creating Interest in your ad by writing up to three benefits for your product or service.

- Looking to create Desire, what can you say about your product or service that will help your ad connect with the reader?

- Your Call to Action could make or break your advertisement. If you are having problems coming up with some ideas of your own, be on the lookout for some effective calls to action that you can tailor to meet your needs.

- Lastly, choose the best from each column in drafting your final ad. Be sure to run the draft past a trusted adviser, and consider their feedback when producing the final version of your ad.

21

Setting Prices

I stumbled across a local newspaper's website and called the Web developer to see if he would like some help redoing their site. I was asked for a quote, and, after some research, I delivered a quote based on my skill level and experience. It has been three weeks now, and I haven't heard back from them. I thought I went about developing the quote the right way, but now I'm wondering if my pricing was ridiculous and they just ignored it completely.

Setting prices is probably one of the most misunderstood elements of small business. Price your products or services too high and you risk losing business to your competition. Price yourself to low and you run the risk of losing money. In any successful business, you want to set prices to cover total costs plus some respectable or healthy level of profit. Before setting your prices, consider these key points:

- Understand the overall market for your product or service.
- Know what channels of distribution exist.
- Find out who your competitors are and the type of businesses they are operating.

If you set prices in a retail business, you want to be familiar with two costs. The first is the cost of acquiring the goods, or the *costs of goods sold* (COGS). The other costs are called *operating expenses,* which can include wages, advertising, salaries, rent, utilities, and office supplies, among other things. In the case of the retail store, one of the key pricing factors is determining your *markup.* Your markup costs go toward covering your operating expenses and some level of profit for yourself and can be either a percentage or some set amount added to the COGS price. This pricing strategy is known as a *cost-based approach.*

A *competition-based approach* can apply to both product and service businesses and is a strategy in which a company sets prices based on those of its competitors. If nonprice considerations are important to customers and there is a certain level of differentiation surrounding your product or service such as customer service, exclusivity, and employee expertise, then it is possible to pursue a *prestige-pricing approach.* This approach allows you to charge higher prices. There is also the *penetration-pricing approach,* which focuses on setting prices low to gain customers and market share.

> *Price too high and you risk losing business; price too low and you risk losing money.*

Many businesses have become more knowledge-based enterprises where primarily one's own expertise is used. In these cases, consultants usually price their services by the hour, depending on their level of expertise. For longer assignments, you might want to consider a complete *project cost.* This project cost includes charges for an adequate number of hours, travel expenses (if necessary), special costs such as equipment or printing, and marketing expenses.

Back to the question presented: It definitely sounds like you're on the right track. With regard to your lack of response from the publication, try not to worry too much about that. It could be that the pricing you submitted frightened the potential client away. But a more likely scenario is that it is simply not the right time for this business to make a financial move—even if it would like to. No worries though. It's simply time to get some feedback on your pricing strategy and then make another phone call.

Setting Your Prices

Setting prices for your company's products or services shouldn't keep you up at night. Try answering the following questions for developing a pricing strategy that works.

- Which of the pricing alternatives discussed do you think would work best for your company's product or service?

- Do the price points you have determined allow your company to realize a reasonable amount of profit?

- Is the pricing that you have selected consistent with the image you are looking to project?

- Are there value-added services (free delivery, customer service, etc.) that you can incorporate into your product or service offering that would justify a higher price?

22

Emerging Markets Provide Answers for Entrepreneurs

As I start this article, I'm half way across the planet in beautiful Ghana, West Africa. Fourteen years ago, I had the amazing opportunity to experience the beauty of Ghana's people, the sites, and the culture. A business graduate at the time, my focus was mostly on the economy and how business worked. What was interesting about my recent trip was how quickly the country's economy has evolved from where it was 14 years ago. After spending the last ten days exploring, it became very clear that the simple, slower paced Ghana that I remembered is a thing of the past. The emerging market of today is defined by a new generation of entrepreneurs who understand that the future of Africa is filled with untold opportunities.

The Rise of Emerging Markets

The Third World countries of yesterday have become the *emerging markets* of today. Emerging market entrepreneurs have found that they can create valuable businesses with very few resources. The Global Entrepreneurship Monitor, which looks at the 54 countries in emerging and developing markets, found that the incidence of entrepreneurship is twice as high in emerging markets as it is in the rest of the developing world. Historically, entrepreneurs in these countries have started 25 percent more companies than their U.S. counterparts and have higher survival rates. These entrepreneurs have become very skilled at identifying opportunities that others don't see or that would deter others because of uncertainty, risk, and scarcity of resources.

Lessons Learned from Ghana

One of the first things that impressed me was the *speed* at which business gets done in Ghana. At one point, my wife realized that we needed a cell phone that would work in the country. While at a festival, she flagged down one of the Vodafone representatives and was able to purchase a cell phone on the spot for $19 GH (cedis, about $13.50 U.S.). It then took only another five minutes to have our new phone activated and loaded with credits (minutes), and we were on our way.

Ghana felt like a nation of 23.8 million entrepreneurs and had a landscape that was covered by roadside shops and street merchants selling everything from apparel, washcloths, and bottles of soda (or pop if you prefer). With the help of major manufacturers—like Procter & Gamble, Coca-Cola, Vodafone, and Nestlé—the country has been able to develop its own creative distribution system that seems to defy logic. Tons of products find their way into the hands of millions of sellers and consumers in a seamless manner—all without sophisticated tracking technology or complicated networks. In addition, Ghanaians have become more marketing savvy highlighting the country's quality of life, tourism, and potential

Emerging market entrepreneurs are creating valuable businesses with very few resources.

business opportunities. Major corporations have begun teaming up with local business owners in an effort to build their brands. Telecom giant Vodafone pays to have its logo painted on entire homes, trotros (local buses), and storefronts.

By the looks of things taking place in many areas of the continent, African businesses are definitely on the rise. A world of opportunities exists for those entrepreneurs around the globe who are willing to take a chance on these and other emerging markets.

Capitalizing on International Opportunities

My amazing market analyst is from China, and her family has a long history of manufacturing in that country. On a recent trip home, she sent me an email with some important information for manufacturing and for conducting business in general in China. Whether your international opportunities lie in China or elsewhere, the following points should provide small businesses with some insight for going global.

- Separate the development of your product into several parts. Find different manufacturers who can make them, and be sure to ask about prices and quantities.

- Never give one manufacturer all of the parts of your products. This could help you to avoid the likelihood of your idea being ripped off.

- Find different manufacturers in different locations such as Shanghai, Shenzhen, Zhengjiang, Ningbo, Hangzhou, and Fujian. This will ensure that production continues if one manufacturers runs into problems.

- Consider finding a printing company in the United States, a company to handle packaging, and a company in both the United States and China to assemble parts if needed.

- Always orders 2 percent to 5 percent extra in case things get damaged in shipping.

23

For Today's Entrepreneurs, It's Hip to Be Square

This year I have committed myself to pushing my technological boundaries. As a lover of traditional media, for me, there's nothing better than grabbing the paper and a cup of coffee to catch up on the day's news. Being partial to old-school media, I'm not easily swayed by the latest gizmos. I think we would all agree the zenith of technology occurred with the invention of Pong and the Betamax machine. With that said, I was surprised when Square caught my attention a couple of years ago. Since that time, I have seen this credit card processing system used everywhere from coffeehouses to county fairs, and it's made me wonder how effective this system would be when applied to the consulting environment.

A History Lesson
The Square credit card reader has positioned itself as the technology that allows you to "Accept payments ... Everywhere." Square is the brainchild of Twitter cofounder Jack Dorsey, who probably just got bored with the success of his media platform and turned his attention to helping small businesses. First introduced in 2009, Square is the complete opposite of the traditional point-of-sales credit systems

that most brick-and-mortar establishments use. Looking to take the place of these bulky readers is Square's miniaturized system, which takes the headache out of credit card processing.

Getting Started

I recently stopped into RadioShack as curiosity got the best of me. After asking a couple of questions and paying my $7.99, I left with a neatly designed "square" package. If you log on to the company's website (www.squareup.com), you can register to have a card reader sent to you free of charge. Because the system works with my iPhone, I first had to download the Square app from iTunes. After reading some product information and recommendations, I completed the download. The entire process took no more than three minutes, at which point I was on to the account setup where I entered basic personal and company contact information.

Determine if company sales will be considerably improved by accepting credit cards.

An Easy Transaction

Not really sure where to begin, I plugged the card reader into my cell phone to attempt a test deposit. The process was as simple as swiping my card, entering an amount, and then authorizing the transaction by using my finger as the pen. I then had a copy of the transaction sent to me via e-mail (I could also have had it sent by text). Having just completed my first Square transaction, I was eager to check my Web-based account, where it immediately showed up in my daily register. There are also areas for checking receipts, payments, and deposits. Despite Square's simplicity, I couldn't shake the feeling that I was missing something. Was there a giant manual that I forgot to read or a four-hour training course that I needed to attend? To my surprise, there was none.

Proceed with Caution

I like Square but I'm not so smitten with the uniqueness of the technology that I would overlook the obvious.

- At 2.75 percent, Square's fees are considered high; lower processing rates exist.
- Square is considered by many as too niche-focused, well suited for start-ups but not for more established companies.
- Consulting company McKinsey estimates the U.S. credit processing industry at $13 billion ($40 billion worldwide). With those types of numbers, Square will continue to face increased competition from copycats and pioneers like PayPal.
- Security concerns persist because if ADP, Google, Citibank, and Zappos can be hacked, then so can a cell phone carrying sensitive credit card information.
- Lastly, customers complain of problems with large transactions not going through and poor customer service.

There's no doubt that Square has caught on, staking its claim in credit processing convenience. Currently, The Entrepreneur Café, LLC, uses PayPal for company transactions, and I don't anticipate making a major shift any time soon. But now that I have actually used the system, I'd hate to find myself in a situation where I needed it for a client and didn't have it available. Square may not become the credit processor of choice for small business owners, but there is no denying that Square is just plain cool!

Evaluating Your Credit Card Processing Options

So you have come to the realization that your business has grown beyond accepting cash and checks from your customers and now needs a system for processing credit cards. Here are some things to think about before taking the leap.

- There are establishments that still operate on a cash-only basis. Determine if your company's sales will be considerably improved by accepting credit cards.

- Download a copy of the Credit Processing Comparison Table from The Entrepreneur Café, LLC, website at www.ecafellc.com/resources. Use the table to do a pro-and-con evaluation of the types of credit processing systems that might work best for your organization.

24

Taking a Step Back
from Business Planning

Recently, I was contacted by a professional who was looking to transition from his career as a road warrior to one that would keep him closer to home. Having some industry insight, he was still concerned that his overall knowledge of the market was lacking and wondered what he should do next. Often times an individual with an idea is encouraged to develop that idea quickly by writing a business plan. I have always looked at businesses like snowflakes with no two being alike. As a result, a business plan might not always be the best first option for a new enterprise. Contrary to my strong belief in business plans, I suggested that we put "the plan" aside in favor of a market feasibility study. A market feasibility study allows us to gain a better understanding of the market potential of a new venture before considerable time and money have been spent.

Reason Behind the Switch

For years now, I have avoided the theory that every new idea needs a lengthy business plan at the outset. In an effort to better serve my clients, I have opted for a more a la carte approach that allows new owners to ease their way into new business development. The reality is that not all business ideas are viable. According to the Small Business Administration, 30 percent of new businesses fail in their first two years; 50 percent fail by year five. The reasons for these failures are numerous, with lack of experience, insufficient capital, and poor location leading the way. With that in mind, what good does it do to invest significant energy into fully developing an idea that may not stand a chance? In the case of my client, the most immediate need was to determine if a significant market existed for his product.

What's Trending?

In conducting a market feasibility study, it's important that you are able to clearly describe your business's products and services. There is also a need to understand what's trending in your industry. Simply put in what general direction is your industry moving. If we examine some popular societal and business trends of the past decade, what comes to mind? Is it the aging of society? The globalization of small business? The rise of social networking? The greening of America? The no-carbs diet? Mobile technology? And the list goes on. When I think about the trends that have driven my own industry and lead to a nation of entrepreneurs, here is what I come up with:

- Increased access to entrepreneurial education
- A shift to a more service-based economy
- Huge technological advances
- A desire for a quality of life change
- Increased international opportunities due to e-commerce

Does your idea look to create or capitalize on a legitimate trend? If so, you could be one step closer to passing the feasibility test, and one step closer to business success.

How Do You Stack Up?

A dangerous thing to hear from a small business owner is, "I don't have any competition." This misconception occurs because the owner hasn't taken the time to investigate who the competition is or because of some perceived superior product or service. This is why conducting a competitive analysis is so important—it allows you to see how you stack up against the competition. I will skip the review of the S.W.O.T. analysis (see article "10: Analysis Is Key to Outwitting the Competition" for more insight). From this

The SBA reports that 30 percent of new businesses fail in their first two years.

review, it is my hope that you will walk away with a better understanding of the strengths, weaknesses, opportunities, and threats your organization faces when dealing with your competitors.

After you have successfully gathered all of your market information and completed your S.W.O.T. analysis, try using that information to develop a competitive statement or a unique selling proposition. The goal of this competitive statement is to clearly and concisely explain what sets you apart from the competition. As a toe-in-water approach to business development, a market feasibility study is not as comprehensive as a business plan is, but it could be exactly what you need to move your next idea forward and save you some headache in the process.

Determine if It's Feasible

Most products and services have a life cycle that begins with strong growth and slows toward the end. Determine where your product or service falls in this process in order to gain a better idea of the market potential.

- Introductory: represents a high growth opportunity

- Maturing: represents a slower growth opportunity

- Saturation: represents a position where the market is crowded and there is little or no growth

- Declining: represents a market that has negative growth or is in significant decline

How is your product differentiated from what is already on the market (in terms of quality and price)? List the five reasons customers will buy from you.

Who are your main competitors in the market, and how do you stack up?

25

Social Entrepreneurs Look to Fundraising to Grow

A 2012 Foundation Survey conducted by *The Chronicles of Philanthropy* reported that seventy-one percent of the foundations surveyed told The Chronicle that their giving would be flat or would drop this year. Since 2001 nonprofits have had to partially set aside their altruistic missions in hopes of finding and maintaining a cash lifeline. For better or worse, today's smaller nonprofits must collaborate and partner with other organizations in order to survive. I recently found myself advising a nonprofit that needed help meeting their financial goals for the upcoming year. With no access to grants and with less sophisticated financial needs my goal was to help them meet their funding needs by creating a gift giving chart.

Why Gift Giving Charts are Important

Gift giving charts are helpful for the following reasons. For starters giving charts serve as a planning tool and helps to determine a pattern of giving and the potential results for a particular campaign. Secondly, giving charts help test donor giving at different giving levels. Lastly, giving charts help to evaluate big picture fundraising efforts, their implementation and effectiveness from year to year. Once you understand how a giving chart helps your financial efforts overall you are ready to set your financial goals.

Determine Your Financial Needs

It's important to start the giving chart with a financial goal in mind. In the case of this organization, we estimated next year's fundraising goals at $60,000. Always looking to plan for the unexpected I raised their goal to $75,000 instead of $60,000 factoring in a 25% contingency. This contingency increases the likelihood of the organization reaching its true funding goal of $60,000. The following steps provide insight for developing a fundraising chart using the needs of this organization as an example.

- Your first gift range should equal **10%** of your goal or $7,500. Try obtaining $3,750 from two different donors.
- Your second giving level should also equal **10%** of your goal or $7,500. Try securing $1,875 from four different donors.
- Your third giving level should equal **15%** of your goal or $11,250. Try securing $937.50 from 12 separate donors.
- Make your fourth giving level equal to **15%** of your goal or $11,250. Try obtaining $625 from 18 separate donors.
- Make your fifth giving level equal to **10%** of your goal or $7,500. Try getting $312.50 from 24 separate donors.
- Make your sixth giving level equal to 20% of your goal or $15,000. Try reaching that goal by getting $125 from 120 separate donors.
- Make your final giving level nominal and equal to **20%** of your goal. Then try getting the lower amount of $30 from your largest base of 500 separate donors.

Fundraising charts usually work best for organizations looking to raise more than $25,000, given the effort that goes into implementing these financial plans. Giving levels and percentages are not set in stone so be sure to adjust to find the numbers that work best for you.

Fundraising is governed by a set of guidelines; for a more information explore the Internal Revenue Service's website. The following are some guidelines to keep in mind when looking to fundraise. Does advertising show the fundraiser is for the clear benefit of the charity? Is the event considered a common business occurrence or a once a year benefit? Lastly, are the majority of the fundraising efforts performed by volunteers with all proceeds used for furthering the charity? Nonprofits have traditionally engaged in fundraising activities as a means of carrying out their charitable purposes. With a little systematic planning you can increase the chances of your fundraising efforts coming off without a hitch.

Smaller nonprofits must collaborate and partner in order to survive.

Developing Your Fundraising Goals

Fundraising is key to the efforts of both for profit and nonprofits alike. Try working through the following exercise to help you reach your financial goals.

- Download a copy of our Fundraising Chart from The Entrepreneur Café, LLC, website at www.ecafellc.com/resources. Take a few moments to examine the gift giving levels and percentages.

- If you are considering fundraising as an option, take time to determine what your fundraising goal is.

- Use the fundraising spreadsheet you downloaded to start experimenting with percentages, gift ranges, and the number of gifts needed to reach that goal.

Share The Entrepreneurial Spirit

The Entrepreneur Café, LLC, has made sharing The Entrepreneurial Spirit a little easier. Purchase a seven-pack of The Entrepreneurial Spirit Lives and give a copy to your closet friends, family members, or business associates. Make The Entrepreneurial Spirit Lives the topic of your next book club selection, or the focus of your next small business training.

7-Pack Bundle   SAVINGS OF **30**%   Price: $79.95

A savings of 30% ($24.98) off the full price of $104.93

Individual / Regular Price   Price: $14.95

For larger wholesale discounts, contact:

The Entrepreneur Café, LLC
715 W. 15th Street
Chicago, IL 60607
phone/fax 877-511-4820
cgray@ecafellc.com
www.ecafellc.com

51274320R00065

Made in the USA
Columbia, SC
15 February 2019